FOUR SIDES OF CALVARY

FOUR SIDES OF CALVARY

Our Lord's Battle On the Cross

*Sermon in a Book Series
Volume 4*

First Edition
©2022 Ken McDonald
All rights reserved

ISBN: 978-1-942769-14-9

All Rights Reserved. No part of this publication may be reproduced, stored in a retrieval system, or transmitted in any form by any means, electronic, mechanical, photocopy, recording, or otherwise, without the prior written permission of the pubisher, except for brief quotations in critical reviews or articles.

All Scripture quotes are from the
King James Authorized Version of 1611

Cover designed by Ken and Terri Lee McDonald
Cover Photo: Shutterstock
www.everywordpublishing.com

Preface

It was a very dark time in my life. Due to over-preaching, my voice was virtually gone. I did not know if I would ever preach again, or even be able to talk. On my way one morning to voice therapy as I was listening to a gospel song, this sermon outline came into my mind. While driving interstate 87 in New Jersey, during the hectic morning rush hour, and steering at times with my knee, I scribbled the outline on a small piece of paper.

This sermon has been a blessing to many and one of my best known sermons. You could say it is one of my brightest sermons, which is strange since it originated in one of my darkest times.

My heart's desire is that you will get a blessing from reading it.

In His Service,
Evangelist Ken McDonald
Jn 9:4

Thank You

I would like to say, Thank you to Pauline, Natalie and my anonymous proof reader. You all have done a great job and have been a big help to the publishing of this book. Lastly, but not least, thank you to my wife, Terri Lee, for her love and support in the ministry.

Four Sides of Calvary

Have you ever asked someone that if they died today do they know that they would go to Heaven? In response they look at you and say, *"Well, the way I see it is..."* and they start talking as if they have gone to seminary. Then in the course of their postulating about eternal things, they say this, *"The way I see it is like this. There is more than one way to look at things so who's to say who's right and wrong?"* And as you speak up and say, *"Well, the Bible says..."* they immediately cut you off by saying, *"You know the Bible can be taken more than one way, and who's to say who's right or wrong."* Not wanting to hear more, they scurry away from the truth to die in their sins and go to Hell.

Having written that though, there is more than one way to look at things, despite truth being not relative.

Four Sides of Calvary

Truth is absolute. Yet in the word of God there are four different views of the life of Jesus Christ. You have Matthew who presents Jesus as the King of the Jews. Then Mark presents Jesus as a servant. Luke presents Jesus as the man, emphasizing the humanity of Christ, which is fitting since Luke was a physician. And lastly John presents Jesus in His deity as the Son of God. Each version of the earthly life of Jesus Christ is true, though none of them are identical.

There are four ways to look at your house. You can be inside looking out. You can be outside looking at your house. You can get above your house and look down on it. Or you can get under your house and look up at it. It is a lot easier to look up at your house if you live in the mountains and have built on the side of a hill. Each view of your house is real and true, but each view is different.

In this book we will look at the four sides of Calvary. First you have the Lord Jesus Christ as He is on the cross looking out. Secondly, you have those around the cross looking on or at the Lord Jesus Christ. Then you have all of Hell looking upward to the Cross. And finally, you have all of Heaven as they look downward on the Cross that day. The four sides of Calvary.

It is a very dark night. But the darkness is more than lack of light for the human eyes physically to see. This is the spiritual darkness that emanates from the evil found strongest in the realm of the principalities and powers and the rulers of the darkness of this world.

Four Sides of Calvary

This night is the night of nights that will go down in all of eternity, for it is the night the Lord Jesus Christ will be arrested, tried and sentenced to die in Golgotha, which is known as, the place of a skull. The depths of hatred for God are on display this night, and yet the heights of love are on display as well. The Creator of all things is allowing Himself to be arrested, sentenced and crucified, while he is innocent, out of love for the world that is lost in sin. It is the most wondrous story of all time, that many still do not understand. For those who do, this story causes them to stop and ponder how unworthy they are, and how great our Lord Jesus Christ is for his love toward you and me.

In Jerusalem, a band of Roman soldiers is given orders to assemble. Standing firm and in formation, they wait for their orders. With torches blazing, the yellow light dances and illuminates the swords, the spears, and the strong, hard faces of the men. Then an officer proudly walks up and stands in front of his men.

Their captain speaks hoarsely gruff and strong. *"You are to follow this man, Judas Iscariot. He knows where to go and he has made an agreement to lead us in the absence of the multitudes to this man called Jesus. The sign he has given us so that we know who to arrest will be the man whom he kisses. That is the man called Jesus. We are to arrest him and bring him to trial tonight."*

> **2 And Judas also, which betrayed him, knew the place: for Jesus ofttimes resorted thither with his disciples. (Jn 18:2)**

Four Sides of Calvary

With Judas leading and the soldiers having swords and staves in hand, they begin to march out to the garden of Gethsemane. Following behind were, "**...the chief priests, and captains of the temple, and the elders...**" (Lk 22:52)

The way before them is dimly lit by the flames of the torches, but lighted well enough for them to see their way. Ahead of them are the eleven disciples and our Lord Jesus Christ. Eight of the disciples are fast asleep on the ground. Peter, James, and John go a little further with the Lord and are very sleepy. They stop, lie down on the ground, and quickly fall asleep.

The Lord Jesus Christ alert and aware, goes by himself about a stone's cast further. Being in great agony, he kneels and prays to His Father, saying, "**O my Father, if it be possible, let this cup pass from me: nevertheless not as I will, but as thou wilt.**" (Mt 26:39) Three times he goes and prays this prayer.

[I find it amazing that even though Jesus Christ was fully God, for the Bible states in Colossians 2 that, "**...in him dwelleth all the fullness of the God head bodily,**" yet while He strode the dusty trails on this earth, he had the human side to him as well. So he prays, "**...not my will, but thine, be done.**" (Lk 22:42) He had a separate will from the Father's will.]

Judas arrives with the mob of soldiers and religious leaders. Without hesitation he comes straight over to Jesus Christ and kisses him.

> And as soon as he was come, he goeth straightway to him, and saith, Master, master; and kissed him. (Mk 14:45)

Jesus then speaks to the soldiers, **"Whom seek ye?"** (Jn 18:4) They answer that they are seeking Jesus of Nazareth. He then answers them and says, **"I am he."**(Jn 18:5) And when He says that, there is a power that comes from Him that pushes the whole group of soldiers and religious leaders backwards, causing them to fall on their backs to the ground.

> **6 As soon then as he had said unto them, I am he, they went backward, and fell to the ground. (Jn 18:6)**

Have you ever wondered what that was all about? It is not every day that someone speaks and the power of his spoken word knocks a band of strong soldiers and religious leaders to the ground.

Here is a chance for Judas and the whole mob to repent. They could have, and should have, said, *"You know what, men? I think this is not just any regular man that we are dealing with. I believe we need to rethink this."* No doubt they have heard of Jesus, for all of Jerusalem is in an uproar because of him. With the religious leaders looking on, then comes the reply, *"An order is an order. We are here to obey our orders, and our orders are to arrest this man, so lets get on with it."*

They then stand up as the Lord asks again, **"Whom seek ye?"**(Jn 18:7) To which they reply again, **"Jesus of Nazareth."** (Jn 18:7) The Lord intercedes for the disciples, and they are let go free.

Watching all that is taking place, and standing by the Lord's side, is Simon Peter. As the soldiers come to arrest Jesus Christ he immediately draws out a sword.

Four Sides of Calvary

All in the same motion, as the sword comes out of its sheath, it's swung horizontally to take off someone's head. That man happens to be Malchus, the high priest's servant.

> **10 Then Simon Peter having a sword drew it, and smote the high priest's servant, and cut off his right ear. The servant's name was Malchus. (Jn 18:10)**

Being young, and having good reflexes, Malchus leans to the side and the sword comes across the side of his head slicing off his ear.

Jesus rebukes Peter, and tells him to put the sword away.

> **11 Then said Jesus unto Peter, Put up thy sword into the sheath: the cup which my Father hath given me, shall I not drink it? (Jn 18:11)**

When the Lord asks Peter about the cup He is to drink, Peter has no idea what Jesus is talking about. But it gives us a glimpse into the mind of our Lord at this time. What is on His mind is doing and finishing the work His Father has given him to accomplish.

> **7 For the Lord GOD will help me; therefore shall I not be confounded: therefore have I set my face like a flint, and I know that I shall not be ashamed. (Is. 50:7)**

> **53 Thinkest thou that I cannot now pray to my Father, and he shall presently give me more than twelve legions of angels?**
>
> **54 But how then shall the scriptures be fulfilled, that thus it must be? (Mt 26:53-54)**

Four Sides of Calvary

After rebuking Peter, Jesus then looks down on the ground, and despite the flickering dim and yellow light He finds the servant's ear. All eyes are now fixed on Jesus Christ as He Picks it up. He then walks over to the servant and puts the bloody ear back on the side of the servants' bloody head.

[51] **And Jesus answered and said, Suffer ye thus far. And he touched his ear, and healed him. (Lk 22:51)**

Again, this is another chance for the mob to repent and go home. But they continue in their wickedness to arrest Jesus Christ and get rid of him.

He is now in the hands of man. He is an innocent prisoner willfully going to die for you and me. And so begins an amazing truth. From Gethsemane to when He is nailed to the cross, almost every time man touches the Lord it causes him to bleed.

Jesus Christ is arrested and quickly taken to court. It is a mockery of a trial. In the process of our Lord's betrayal, they place a crown of thorns upon His head and beat it down onto His brow. Sharp thorns pierce the skin of His head. Blood begins to flow down His neck, behind His ears, into His eyes and drips off His chin.

Those thorns with which He is pierced were grown by Him. He watered them with rain, caused the sun to shine so they would grow, all the while knowing they would pierce His own brow one day.

That thorny, painful crown of mockery encircles the head and the mind of God. Beaten down upon His head by wicked men with wicked minds, that thorny crown wraps around a holy mind which never has a wicked thought. It never has an evil imagination. It is the mind of God; pure, perfect and right. Yet, it is surrounded by thorns that grew as a result of a curse placed upon nature.

You see, the One wearing that crown of thorns is the One who cursed the ground. Genesis 3 states that the ground would bring forth thorns and thistles.

> **17 And unto Adam he said, Because thou hast hearkened unto the voice of thy wife, and hast eaten of the tree, of which I commanded thee, saying, Thou shalt not eat of it: cursed is the ground for thy sake; in sorrow shalt thou eat of it all the days of thy life;**
>
> **18 Thorns also and thistles shall it bring forth to thee; and thou shalt eat the herb of the field; (Gn 3:17-18)**

Jesus is not only paying for my sins and your sins, but He is making an atonement for all of nature as well. No, "nature" did not, and has not sinned against God like man has. Some claim that if God is God then He could have stopped the suffering. They claim it's not right that He would not only allow suffering in creation, but also cause it.

Although God never has and never will do wrong, yet he paid the price for creation as well. When all is done and time is no more, the lost will stand before God at the Great White Throne Judgement. They may accuse God of not being just, but after Calvary they will not have the slightest possibility of credibility to their argument.

In mockery, the soldiers bow the knee before him. They smite him on the face while he is blindfolded. With laughter inspired by devils within them, they contemptuously ask, *"Who smote thee?"* One day though, they will not laugh; for one day they will stand naked and ashamed before this very One. They will bow the knee and confess that Jesus is Lord to the glory of God the Father.

The torments continue as the mockers begin to pull and rip the beard off His face.

> **6 I gave my back to the smiters, and my cheeks to them that plucked off the hair: I hid not my face from shame and spitting. (Is 50:6)**

As they pull His beard out, blood begins to flow from around His lips. Lips that have never told a lie. Lips that have never been used in an ungodly way. They are lips that speak the holy words of God. Some of those words we have in the Bible, and many Bibles have those words written in red ink. Words which tell us sinners how we can know that we are are going to Heaven when we die. We must be born again. There are no sweeter words to a sinner's ear than the words of Jesus. **"...I am come that they might have life, and that they might have it more abundantly."** (Jn. 10:10b) The blood continues to flow and fall from the head of the Creator of the universe.

The torture continues as the soldiers begin to whip the Lord Jesus Christ. That scourge has strands of leather with shards of metal and bone attached to those strands. The scourge is designed to cut the flesh and cause great pain and bleeding.

A big burly man steps up with a crazed grin on his face. His eyes are wide open and glaring. Swinging the weapon of torture with glee, the first slash is struck across our Lord's back. The leather strands seem to stick to His back as the pointed shards sink into His skin. After a slight moment of hesitation the man pulls the scourge across our Lord's back. For a split second there are white streaks across the back of Jesus Christ, but then those white streaks turn a deep, dark red as they fill up with God's blood.

> [3] **The plowers plowed upon my back: they made long their furrows. (Ps 129:3)**

Over and over the jagged leather laces rip grooves across His back, His stomach, arms and legs, as the blood flows from Immanuel's veins. Blood that is paying the price for my sins and your sins.

The torture has taken all night, and now the morning dawns. The soldiers lead Jesus Christ out to Calvary, the place of a skull. Bearing His cross Jesus trods the way leaving behind Him a trail of blood.

Some claim Simon, the Cyrene, carries the cross at the start but cannot make it all the way. So Jesus finishes the trek, carrying His cross out to Calvary. The Catholics have it the other way around and claim that Jesus could only go part way and then collapses. Simon is standing close by and is forced by the Roman soldiers to carry the cross for Jesus the rest of the way to Golgotha.

³² And as they came out, they found a man of Cyrene, Simon by name: him they compelled to bear his cross. (Mt 27:32)

¹⁷ And he bearing his cross went forth into a place called the place of a skull, which is called in the Hebrew Golgotha... (Jn 19:17)

At first I believed the Catholic version, but the more I closely studied it out, it appears that Simon does not make it. Jesus himself finishes the trek. John plainly states that Jesus is bearing His cross "**into**" Golgotha. With Jesus' physical body of flesh shredded the way it was, it would be impossible for any mortal man to do what He did. But Jesus is no mortal man. Fully man, yes! But also fully God! He bore His cross into Golgotha.

It is now the third hour Jewish time, which is 9:00 a.m. Gentile time. It is the 14th of Abib, Wednesday morning. The day is not Friday morning. It is Wednesday morning. At the risk of running a rabbit trail, let me just give a brief explanation of why the crucifixion took place on Wednesday. (See chart for further explanation.)

Jesus said that He would be three days and three nights in the heart of the earth. We know He came up Sunday morning. Count backwards, Saturday night and Saturday day is one day. Friday night and Friday day are two days. Thursday night, and Thursday day are three days. Guess what, you are at Wednesday 9:00 a.m.

Remember also that the 15th of Abib, the day after

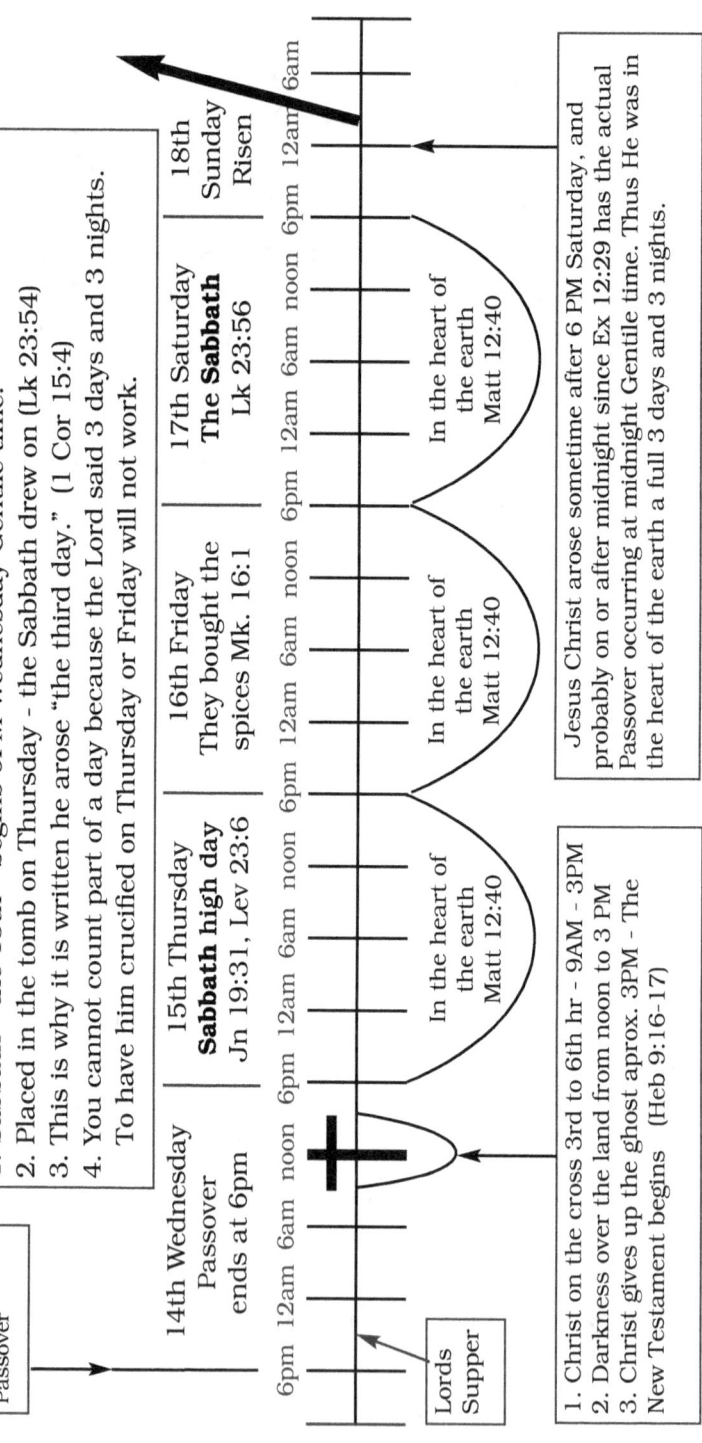

Four Sides of Calvary

the Passover was a special Sabbath that is referred to in John 19:31 as "...an high day."

> ⁵ In the fourteenth day of the first month at even is the LORD'S passover.
>
> ⁶ And on the fifteenth day of the same month is the feast of unleavened bread unto the LORD: seven days ye must eat unleavened bread.
>
> ⁷ In the first day ye shall have an holy convocation: ye shall do no servile work therein. (Lv 23:6-7)

It was a Sabbath, so you have Thursday a special high day Sabbath, and then you have Saturday the Sabbath "...according to the commandment" (Lk 23:56) referring to the fourth commandment of the Ten Commandments of Exodus 20. This is a brief explanation, but enough to show that the Crucifixion took place on Wednesday morning.

As He arrives at Calvary, Jesus lets go of the cross and it slams flat on the ground. He looks down at it as blood drips off His nose and chin. The soldiers, who have seen a lot of blood in their day, stare at Him in astonishment, for they have never seen anyone so torn and bloody yet still be alive.

> ¹⁴ As many were astonied at thee; his visage was so marred more than any man, and his form more than the sons of men...
> (Is 52:14)

The soldiers are even more astonished with Jesus as they witness what he does next. They watch in wonder

Four Sides of Calvary

as this bloody man standing in front of them, willingly lays down on the cross with His back against it as He looks up to Heaven. Jesus stretches out his bloody arms and relaxes His wrists. Astonished again, they look at each other as if to say, I have never seen that before!

Though surprised, one of the soldiers grabs a large iron nail and hammers it through His hand at what we would call the wrist.

How do we know that? Well, if it were in the palm of the hand, the nail would rip out as He hung on the cross.

When Rebekah is given bracelets in Genesis 24:30, she puts them upon her hands, thus showing that the wrist is part of the hand according to:

> ^{30} **And it came to pass, when he saw the earring and bracelets upon his sister's hands...** (Gn 24:30)

Each hand is nailed to the cross, and then, with one foot on top of the other, one nail is hammered through both of His feet. Once again the veins are cruelly opened and God's blood (Acts 20:28) flows from His hands and feet. Hands that healed the blind, lifted up the dead, calmed the raging sea, and washed the disciples feet.

There on Calvary, Wednesday morning at 9:00 a.m., the Creator of the universe, who had come to earth as a man, is lifted up upon a rugged wooden cross. The cross slides down into its designated hole and hits the bottom with a deep thud. His bloody body jerks from it all, as Jesus hangs on a cross dying for you and me. Why? Because He loves you. Why? Because He does not want to see anyone go to Hell, so He paid for all of our sins. Why? Because it was His Father's will. Why? Because the true God of the universe is good.

There, on the cross. Behold the man!

> Oh sacred head now wounded
> With grief and shame weighed down
> Now scornfully surrounded
> With thorns thy only crown
>
> How pale thou art with anguish
> With sore abuse and scorn
> How does that visage languish
> Which once was bright as morn
>
> (From the Hymn, O Sacred Head: circa 1200 AD)

In spite of the blood loss, Jesus is awake and aware of all that is going on around Him. There are two other malefactors being crucified as well. One on His right, and the other on His left.

The soldiers have likely seen quite a few crucifixions. They have seen naked mangled bodies on crosses before, but this day is different. They can not keep their eyes off of that One in the middle. **"And sitting down they watched Him there..."** (Mt 27:36) They have never seen a body that mangled, that shredded and bloody.

Relatives of the other two men are nearby crying. Even though they are broken over their loved ones dying that day, their eyes are drawn back to stare at the One in the middle. Jesus is aware of this.

> ^{17} I may tell all my bones: they look and stare upon me. (Ps 22:17)

Jesus is being openly humiliated and mocked by the gloating chief priests, scribes and elders as they gather around the three crosses. The naked, bloody red, black and blue, body of Jesus Christ is such that everyone present that day could not keep from staring.

In those early minutes of his six hours upon the cross, Jesus looks out and begins to speak. What does He say?

> ^{34} ...Father, forgive them; for they know not what they do. (Lk 23:34)

Remember this, that as you read about Jesus Christ, you are getting a glimpse of what God is like. You are seeing what makes God angry, and what God loves. You are seeing the personification of God in the man Jesus Christ. In Luke 23:34, you see the greatest example of intercession. Jesus Christ is interceding for His enemies. He is praying for His Father to forgive them for what they have done to Him. Behold the man! Behold that picture of the God of the universe.

> ^{12} Therefore will I divide him a portion with the great, and he shall divide the spoil with the strong; because he hath poured out his soul unto death: and he was numbered with the transgressors; and he bare the sin of many, and made intercession for the transgressors. (Is 53:12)

Four Sides of Calvary

There is not another religious book on earth that portrays any god like this! The gods of the heathen hold absolute power over their subjects. The people cower in fear and trembling, afraid they might make their god angry. They throw babies in rivers, burn their babies in fires, and live in extreme fear of their gods. But in the Bible, here is a completely different picture of the true God of all of creation. He is wrongfully being murdered. He has the power to call twelve legions of angels to deliver Himself from the pain and death of the crucifixion. Yet He prays to his Father to forgive them, **"...for they know not what they do."**

I am reminded of a story I heard a preacher tell. Though it was fairly cold, this preacher was out on the streets at night talking to whomever he could about the Lord Jesus Christ. He noticed a man walking down the sidewalk towards him, so he spoke to the man when he got close. The man stopped and listened to this preacher as he told him how he could have forgiveness and go to Heaven when he died. As the preacher continued the man spoke up and said, *"Preacher, my wife is down there in that house with another man right now, and I am going down there to kill them both."* He pulled out a revolver that he had in his coat pocket. As the preacher talked to him, the man became more furious and seemed more determined that he was going to go kill them both.

In a flash of inspiration, the Lord gave the preacher a thought that might help this man repent from what he was determined to do. With his Bible open, the preacher showed him Jesus Christ on the cross praying, **"Father, forgive them, for they know not what they do."** He said to the man, *"Do you see that? Jesus Christ is a better man dying, than you are living."* The man looked at the preacher and said, *"I suppose you're right."* He handed his gun to the preacher and walked back to where he had come from.

On the cross that day God is loving His enemies. There is no other God like that! It is here at Calvary you will behold the greatest love the world has, and ever will have the opportunity to see.

This is early in the Crucifixion time frame. Probably within the first hour between 9AM and 10AM. After He prays for His enemies, Jesus then sees Mary, His earthly mother. She is not the "mother of God," she is the earthly mother of the man Jesus. He sees her with the apostle John by her side. He then says to Mary, **"Woman, behold thy son!"** (Jn 19:26) And then He says to John, **"Behold thy mother! And from that hour that disciple took her unto his own home."** (Jn 19:27) From that time forth John took care of Mary.

Then a great crowd of people gather around the cross. People are mocking Him. A voice rings out, as one of the chief priests from the crowd laughingly yells out, **"He saved others; himself he cannot save."** (Mt 27:42) And yet it is so true, for He came to save sinners. He was dying for them. The death of Jesus Christ is the greatest selfless act that ever was. He did not come to save Himself, He came to save sinners.

Others walked by and spit on Him, while others spit

Four Sides of Calvary

in His face. (The Cross was not as high as is often portrayed in paintings.)

> ^{6} I gave my back to the smiters, and my cheeks to them that plucked off the hair: I hid not my face from shame and spitting. (Is 50:6)

During the first hour of the Crucifixion, the two thieves are reviling Him as well.

> ^{43} He trusted in God; let him deliver him now, if he will have him: for he said, I am the Son of God.
>
> ^{44} The thieves also, which were crucified with him, cast the same in his teeth. (Mt 27:43-44)

The soldiers sit down and watch Him as they gamble for His clothes. To them it is just another day, except they could not keep from looking up at that One in the middle. It seems everyone that day stared at the One in the middle.

> ^{36} **And sitting down they watched him there...** (Mt 27:36)

It is strange to imagine that a little ways off in Jerusalem, people are going about their normal every day business. Some are sweeping and cleaning their houses. Men are going to work after breakfast like any other day. The sun is shining. Birds are chirping and flying in the sky while dogs are barking off in the distance. But there on Calvary that day, the Son of God is laying down His life for the sins of the whole world.

> ²⁹ Behold the Lamb of God, which taketh away the sin of the world. (Jn 1:29)
>
> ¹⁷ I may tell all my bones: they look and stare upon me. (Ps 22:17)

Jesus is aware of the people staring at Him. But as the people stare at Him, another group of creatures are watching and staring. Down, way down in the bottomless pit of Hell, the devils look up to watch as the Lamb of God suffers, bleeds, and dies. Their desire is to stop Him, for He is sealing their doom for all eternity. What can they do? Desperation takes hold in the bottomless pit of Hell. A spirit slithers up to one of the soldiers who is sitting beside the cross and whispers in his ear, *"Give Him something to drink."*

The soldier then unknowingly led by an unclean spirit, stood up and said to the others, *"I think I'll give Him something to drink."* They assumed he was referring to Jesus, the One in the middle.

> ²¹ They gave me also gall for my meat; and in my thirst they gave me vinegar to drink. (Ps 69:21)

Dipping some hyssop into a dirty pail of vinegar, myrrh, and gall, he sticks the sponge-like hyssop on the end of his spear and raises it up to the bloody mouth of Jesus Christ. Jesus tastes it, turns His head to the side and spits it out.

> ³⁴ They gave him vinegar to drink mingled with gall: and when he had tasted thereof, he would not drink. (Mt 27:34)

Four Sides of Calvary

Shouts of joy and praise to the Lamb of God ring out in Paradise as the saved saints of old cheer for the Lord Jesus Christ. Across the great gulf into the hot, dark, fiery place of Hell, the eternally damned souls look up and carefully watch as the dirty, bitter, gall and vinegar slop is offered, but Jesus would not drink. A hate-filled, defeated, screaming cry echoes through the flaming black pit of Hell. Why?

Because Jesus Christ is the Lamb of God. According to the book of Exodus, when the Passover lamb is to be roasted, it was not allowed to be sodden at all with water.

> [9] **Eat not of it raw, nor sodden at all with water, but roast with fire; his head with his legs, and with the purtenance thereof. (Ex 12:9)**
>
> [14] **...for the LORD our God hath put us to silence, and given us water of gall to drink, because we have sinned against the LORD. (Jer 8:14)**
>
> [15] **...Behold, I will feed them, even this people, with wormwood, and give them water of gall to drink. (Jer 9:15)**
>
> [15] **...make them drink the water of gall: for from the prophets of Jerusalem is profaneness gone forth into all the land. (Jer 23:15)**

According to Luke 23:36, they were mocking him by offering him the vinegar mingled with gall. In the gall and vinegar was water. If he would have drunk that, it

Four Sides of Calvary

would have broken Scripture and thus the devils would have won the battle.

The goal of the devils of Hell that day, allowed by the permissive will of God, was to attempt to get Jesus Christ to break Scripture or to altogether quit. To quit would be to leave His mortality and to "switch over" to His infinite powers of God. In doing this He would have broken scripture, and thus fail in completing the Father's will. Completing the Father's will for His life was the Lord Jesus Christ's main desire while on this earth as a man. It ought to be your desire as well.

Just as the principalities and powers and the rulers of the darkness of this world, and the spiritual wickedness in high places (Eph 6:12) are trying to defeat Jesus Christ this day, so too Jesus Christ is challenging Satan and all the powers of Hell as he suffers, bleeds and lays down His life. For all to see, as Jesus Christ hangs on the cross this day, He is making a show of the wickedness in high places openly. In other words, it is not even a contest. We would say he is showing them up.

> [14] **Blotting out the handwriting of ordinances that was against us, which was contrary to us, and took it out of the way, nailing it to his cross;**
>
> [15] **And having spoiled principalities and powers, he made a shew of them openly, triumphing over them in it. (Col 2:14-15)**

Notice the following scripture as well. The following is Jesus Christ challenging Lucifer directly.

⁵ The Lord GOD hath opened mine ear, and I was not rebellious, neither turned away back.

⁶ I gave my back to the smiters, and my cheeks to them that plucked off the hair: I hid not my face from shame and spitting.

⁷ For the Lord GOD will help me; therefore shall I not be confounded: therefore have I set my face like a flint, and I know that I shall not be ashamed.

⁸ He is near that justifieth me; who will contend with me? let us stand together: who is mine adversary? let him come near to me.
(Is 50:5-8)

Notice verse 6 for the context. It is obviously a reference to Jesus Christ and his suffering. This verse is prophetic in regard to the torture and mocking that occurred prior to being lifted up on the cross. This prophecy is fulfilled when these things happened to Jesus Christ.

In verse 7 you will notice "**...I have set my face like a flint.**" From Gethsemane on, Jesus Christ is determined to go to the cross. As He prayed in the garden, He wrestled and prayed that the cross might be removed. But Jesus always ended the prayer with, "**...not my will but thine be done.**" (Lk 22:42) After the third time praying, He was ready. He set His face like a flint. There was no turning back.

Now we come to verse 8, an amazing verse of scripture! "**Who will contend with me?**" There is a contention that is going to take place. A battle, you could say. It is a battle between Jesus Christ and Lucifer.

"**Let us stand together: who is mine adversary?**" Who was the adversary of Jesus Christ? No doubt it was Satan i.e., Lucifer. The true Light is challenging the false light. Lucifer means to bring light. (Webster 1913) "**...Let him come near to me.**" vs 8 In so many words Jesus Christ is saying to Satan, *"Here is your chance. Bring it on and give me your best shot."* And so a battle began that day at Calvary. A battle of good and evil. Yet, the battle was never in doubt as to whom was going to win. It was a "battle" to show that Jesus Christ is the King of Heaven and earth.

You might remember that Jesus said at the end of the gospel of Matthew, "**All power is given unto me in heaven and in earth.**" (Matt 28:18) Any power that Satan has in this age has been given to him by Jesus Christ. But this brings up an interesting thought. If Satan gets his power from Jesus Christ, and knows from the word of God that he is going to lose, then why does he fight? What's more is that Satan lost the fight at Calvary. Not only there, but the victory was confirmed when Jesus Christ arose from the grave. So why does he keep fighting and pressing on?

The answer to that is found in the following verse.

[13] **But exhort one another daily, while it is called To day; lest any of you be hardened through the deceitfulness of sin. (Heb 3:13)**

Sin is deceptive and Satan is the embodiment of sin.

Four Sides of Calvary

In the tribulation, he is referred to as the **"man of sin,"** and **"the son of perdition."** (2 Thes 2:3) Satan believes that he will win, and probably believes that he is winning right now. He does not believe the word of God, he merely knows what the Bible says, but He does not believe it.

It is similar to gambling, though when you are fighting God, you will never win. But person after person has become involved in gambling, and they cannot quit. It gets ahold of them like a drug addiction. They start believing, *"Maybe this one and I'll be rich. Maybe this next one. Sooner or later the odds will go my way."* On and on they go until they have nothing left.

Satan goes on and on in his deception. Though it has already been demonstrated 2000 years ago when Jesus Christ beat him, and it wasn't even a serious challenge. Jesus Christ made a show of him openly.

On the cross that day, the Lord Jesus Christ looks out at all around, **"...despising the shame."** (Heb 12:2) **"...they look and stare upon me."** (Ps 22:17)

The people gather around and mock, laughing at and spitting upon him. The soldiers sit and watch him.

All of Hell looks upward and watch as they, allowed by God, try to cause Jesus Christ to "slip up" and fail. But He is making a show of them openly.

> [14] **Blotting out the handwriting of ordinances that was against us, which was contrary to us, and took it out of the way, nailing it to his cross;**
>
> [15] **And having spoiled principalities and**

> powers, he made a shew of them openly, triumphing over them in it. (Col 2:14-15)

All of Heaven watches with great wonder from above. You see, the angels do not understand what is happening. An angel will never be able to sing, *"Redeemed, how I love to proclaim it. Redeemed by the blood of the Lamb."* While the suffering of the Lamb of God takes place this day, they do not understand what is happening. The One that they have proclaimed in praise and worship to, *"Holy, Holy, Holy,"* is now being crucified when He does not deserve it. How can this be?

There is an old hymn titled Crown Him with Many Crowns, and in that song are the words:

Crown Him the Lord of love!
Behold His hands and side,
Rich wounds, yet visible above,
In beauty glorified:
No angel in the sky
Can fully bear that sight,
But downward bends his wondering eye
At mysteries so bright!

In 1 Peter 1 is recorded the following that shows the angels desire to look into these things.

> [10] **Of which salvation the prophets have enquired and searched diligently, who prophesied of the grace that should come unto you:**
>
> [11] **Searching what, or what manner of time**

> the Spirit of Christ which was in them did signify, when it testified beforehand the sufferings of Christ, and the glory that should follow.
>
> ^{12} Unto whom it was revealed, that not unto themselves, but unto us they did minister the things, which are now reported unto you by them that have preached the gospel unto you with the Holy Ghost sent down from heaven; which things the angels desire to look into. (1 Pt 1:10-12)

As you can see from verse 12, the angels desire to look into the sufferings of Christ, His burial, His resurrection, and the glory that follows. Where do they look? In the word of God. Just as they seek to understand these things, so too that day on Calvary they do not understand what is happening. They watch from Heaven as the Lord of Heaven is wrongfully crucified. The One that all of Heaven worships is now being rejected, mocked, shamefully treated, and crucified.

The angels, including Michael, Gabriel, and all the host of Heaven, watch as Jesus is hanging from the cross. The Father is watching as well, for the Bible says, **"He shall see of the travail of his soul..."** (Is 53:11) Then one of the angels comes over and says to the Father, *"Let me go. Father, let me go and I will deliver him."* Yet those angels know that Jesus has the power to deliver Himself. Oh yes, the angels are greatly perplexed as they watched the Lamb of God be crucified.

Four Sides of Calvary

As I said, and keep in mind that God the Father is watching from Heaven, beholding the travail of the soul of Jesus Christ. I wonder if Darius the king in Daniel 6 is a picture of the Father? Daniel 6 is the story of Daniel in the lions' den. There is no doubt that in this story Daniel is a type of Jesus Christ.

Daniel was betrayed to be killed. Jesus Christ was also betrayed to be killed. Daniel was innocent, and Jesus Christ was innocent. Daniel was a picture of the death, burial and resurrection of Jesus Christ. He was cast into the den of lions - death. The pit was sealed - burial. And the next day he came out alive - resurrection. (This is a type. It was not three days and three nights, but it is still a type.)

Knowing that this is a type of the death, burial and resurrection, take a look at King Darius. Even as king, Darius is subject to the words of the Law.

> ^{16} Then the king commanded, and they brought Daniel, and cast him into the den of lions. Now the king spake and said unto Daniel, Thy God whom thou servest continually, he will deliver thee.
>
> ^{17} And a stone was brought, and laid upon the mouth of the den; and the king sealed it with his own signet, and with the signet of his lords; that the purpose might not be changed concerning Daniel.
>
> ^{18} Then the king went to his palace, and passed the night fasting: neither were instruments of musick brought before him: and his sleep went from him. (Dn 6:16-18)

It is obvious King Darius is upset and concerned for Daniel. He spends the night fasting and does not sleep. How far can you press the type? I do not know for sure.

Does God know all things? Of course He does. Does He know the suffering that Jesus is going to go through, not only on the cross, but also as He becomes sin for us? Of course He does.

Perhaps, in the garden of Gethsemane as Jesus begins to pray, it moves the Father as He listens to the prayer. (Please understand, I am only wondering and I do not teach this as doctrine.) But I wonder if the Father begins to run His mind through the Scriptures, looking for a way out. But how? How could He run His mind through the Scriptures when He instantly knows all the scriptures for He is the embodiment of those Scriptures? Yet, the Scriptures are infinite, just like Him. I do not know, but perhaps He looked for a way his Son could get out of it all. He searches, muses, and replies to Jesus Christ, *"You must go all the way."* Jesus replies, *"Nevertheless, not my will but thine be done."*

His heart is still heavy and burdened, so Jesus prays yet again in agony. He sweats as it were great drops of blood. And it moves the heart of His Father. Again the Father comes back with the same answer, and Jesus gives back the same reply.

And then Jesus prays again, *"Please, let this cup pass from me."* To this the Father may have replied, *"If You don't go all the way to the cross, then the souls in Paradise will never get out. And the sinners to be born*

Four Sides of Calvary

will never be saved, and You will never have a bride. And if You don't go all the way to the cross, then We will have never demonstrated the greatest picture of love the world has ever known. And We will never have souls in Heaven who have freely chosen us. Jesus, my beloved Son, it is My will that You go all the way and pay the price for their sins. It is My will for You to show the greatest love for all eternity."

Jesus replied, "Father, if that is Your will, then Thy will be done."

And from Heaven the Father watches as His Son is crucified.

The first hour has passed and many of the mockers have left. Perhaps a few relatives of the other two malefactors are still there. But who do we know is there? Though the Bible says "**...they all forsook him and fled,**" (Mk 14:50) yet some of the disciples return and are in the area. John went into the palace of the high priest. He was known by the high priest. He then returned to the door of the palace and encouraged Peter to enter as well. Of course, this was before the crucifixion.

We know Peter is there according to the following verse.

> [1] **The elders which are among you I exhort, who am also an elder, and a witness of the sufferings of Christ, and also a partaker of the glory that shall be reveal...** (1 Pt 5:1)

We know John is there along with Mary, the earthly mother of Jesus. Mary Magdalene is also there.

> ⁴⁰ There were also women looking on afar off: among whom was Mary Magdalene, and Mary the mother of James the less and of Joses, and Salome... (Mk 15:40)

We also know they did not understand what was happening. The following verse shows Jesus opened their understanding of the Scriptures after He was risen from the dead.

> ⁴⁵ Then opened he their understanding, that they might understand the scriptures, (Lk 24:45)

So at this point, the disciples that are present at Calvary, do not understand what is happening, or why it is happening.

Was there anybody there that day that understood what was happening? The angels didn't understand. The disciples didn't understand. If there was anyone that day who would've understood what was happening, it would have been Mary, the sister of Martha, and there is no record of her even being present at Calvary that day.

> ³ Then took Mary a pound of ointment of spikenard, very costly, and anointed the feet of Jesus, and wiped his feet with her hair: and the house was filled with the odour of the ointment. (Jn 12:3)
>
> ⁷ Then said Jesus, Let her alone: against the day of my burying hath she kept this. (Jn 12:7)

Four Sides of Calvary

If there was anyone who understood what was happening that day it would've been Mary. She had kept the ointment for His burial. How did she know? She sat at His feet and listened to Him teach her the word of God, while Martha was busy in the kitchen.

The first three hours of our Lord's suffering is with the sun shining brightly, and birds that circle in the sky waiting for a meal. Moans and groans are heard from the other two men being crucified. The soldiers are still sitting there talking amongst themselves, but their eyes, though not as often, keep drifting back to that One in the middle.

Mary Magdalene is weeping with Mary as they hug each other and cry. Then Mary Magdalene comes over to Peter and speaks to him, with a broken but tender voice. Tracks of tears are seen on her cheeks as she continues to weep. She asks, *"Peter, what's happening? Why is this happening?"* Tearfully and thoughtfully she continues, *"He...He gave me a new life. I was a miserable harlot, and Jesus delivered me from the bondage. Peter, you know as much as anyone, He...He doesn't deserve this. Peter why?"*

The whole time Mary Magdalene is talking to Peter he just stands there staring at Jesus Christ on the cross. He is listening to her, and yet he is going over in his mind the memories of the previous three and a half years, as if searching for an answer but not able to find one. As she continues to ask Peter why, he then faintly speaks to her almost in a whisper, though still staring at the cross: *"I walked on the water with Him."*

Four Sides of Calvary

Mary Magdalene stops, and is confused by Peter's reply, so she asks, *"What?"*

Peter, with more focus in his mind now speaks a little more clearly to her, *"I walked on the water with Him. It was just Him and me on the sea of Galilee. I began to sink and He lifted me up out of the water. I've never felt such strength from a man as I did that day."* Peter then turns and looks into Mary Magdalenes eyes and softly says with a sense of confusion, *"I don't know Mary. I… I don't know."*

Frustrated and confused Peter then turns to John, who is on the other side of him, also gazing intently at Jesus Christ as he hangs upon the cross.

With a most bewildered sounding voice, Peter asks, *"John, why? You know He doesn't deserve this. I remember saying, 'Thou art the Christ,' remember John? We were convinced that He was the Messiah, and somehow I still want to believe He is, but….I…I….don't know. John, you were closer than any of us to Him. Why? Why is this happening?"*

John stares at the cross as if he were day dreaming. Peter is about to ask him if he is alright when John speaks low as if dazed. Almost as if he wis talking to himself, while still facing the cross,

John, softly whispers, *"I heard his heart beat."*

Peter wasn't sure of what John said so he asks him, *"What?"*

John, still staring at the cross, answers again, *"I heard his heart beat."*

Peter is still confused, so John turns and looks at him.

Four Sides of Calvary

John realizing Peter is confused, then says to him, *"You remember, last night? When we were having the Passover feast, I was leaning on His breast?"*

Peter, now understanding what John is saying, quickly responds, *"Oh...Oh Yeah."*

As his mind replays the pleasant memory, John says it again, *"I heard his heart beat."*

Peter, with some impatience asks, *"John, why is this happening? What is going on? Mary asked me and I told her I don't know."*

John then turning back to look at Jesus on the cross says quietly, *"I don't know either."*

At the foot of the cross their minds are filled with confusion. Their hearts are filled with sorrow. Their hopes and joys have been dashed. To them the light of their lives is being snuffed out and He doesn't deserve what He is getting. Their light is turning to darkness. Little do they know of the darkness that is about to overtake them.

11:00 a.m. passes, and it is now almost 12:00 noon. Jesus has been silent for over two hours.

About 11:55 a.m., one of the thieves speaks. As he speaks, he continues to rail on Jesus Christ.

> [39] **And one of the malefactors which were hanged railed on him, saying, If thou be Christ, save thyself and us.**
>
> [40] **But the other answering rebuked him, saying, Dost not thou fear God, seeing thou art in the same condemnation?**
>
> [41] **And we indeed justly; for we receive the**

due reward of our deeds: but this man hath done nothing amiss.

⁴² And he said unto Jesus, Lord, remember me when thou comest into thy kingdom.

⁴³ And Jesus said unto him, Verily I say unto thee, To day shalt thou be with me in paradise.

⁴⁴ ¶ And it was about the sixth hour, and there was a darkness over all the earth until the ninth hour. (Lk 23:39-44)

Now something has happened to the other thief. Instead of agreeing and railing on Jesus with the other malefactor, he is defending Jesus Christ. He now condemns himself. As he speaks, his voice is hoarse, his strength is weakening, and his tongue is swelling. With determination and purpose he says, "**...we indeed justly; for we receive the due reward of our deeds: but this man hath done nothing amiss.**" (Lk 23:41)

Do you want to make it to Heaven? Do you want to be right with God? You need to be willing to condemn yourself. That is what mortal, sinful, prideful man does not want to do. He does not want to admit the problem is himself. As the old song says, *"It's me, it's me, it's me, oh Lord, standin' in the need of prayer. Not my brother, not my sister, but it's me, oh Lord, standin' in the need of prayer!"* The problem is me!

One of the thieves has been thinking for three hours. Perhaps he has heard of Jesus. Chances are he has. And he may have heard the accusations heaped upon the Lord. He heard the mockers and what they spoke, and then he heard Jesus say, **"Father, forgive them; for they know not what they do."** These words of forgiveness, along with the public accusations keep ringing in his ears and more importantly in his heart. He had been angry and accusing along with the other thief, yet Jesus is not angry and asks God to forgive them. This must have troubled him. No doubt, it did make him think and search his own heart.

Then, at about 11:55 a.m., the thief now speaks up. It is almost as if when he condemns himself a light comes on. He realizes who Jesus Christ really is, for he says, **"Lord."** When you can justly condemn yourself and confess that Jesus is the Lord, you are on your way to being forgiven. He says, **"...Lord, remember me when thou comest into thy kingdom."** (Lk 23:42)

Think about this. If there was ever a time when Jesus Christ would have been too busy for someone, it would have been then. He is right in the middle of making the atonement. He is in great physical pain. It would not have been a surprise if He said to the thief, *"Not now, I'm busy."* But that is not who our Lord Jesus Christ is. He is a Saviour that is concerned with individuals. He is concerned about you!

Have you ever wondered if Jesus was just too busy to be concerned with you or your silly little prayer? I have! But it is a great comfort to know that if Jesus had time to respond to a guilty dying thief, then he has the time, and the heart, to hear my prayers and help me. Dear reader, please remember that there is no prayer too small for Jesus Christ. You usually hear that there is

Four Sides of Calvary

no prayer too big for Jesus Christ. But he is concerned about all of your cares. You are to cast all of your cares upon him, for "**...He careth for you.**" (1 Pt 5:7) And when he says, "**You,**" he means you.

Right there, in the middle of dying for you and me, a guilty thief speaks to Jesus Christ, and the Lord pays some attention to him. You know, the day you called upon Jesus Christ to save you, He payed attention to you. Think about this. God did something He would not have done, if you had not prayed. Did you get that? When you prayed, the Creator of the universe did something He would not have done, if you had not asked.

So this dying thief asks the Lord Jesus Christ to remember him, and Jesus responds by telling him, "**To day shalt thou be with me in Paradise.**" (Lk 23:43) With those spoken words, that dying thief turned his head back, and a groan of relief was heard as peace flooded his soul.

It is now 12:00 noon.

> ^{44} **And it was about the sixth hour, and there was a darkness over all the earth until the ninth hour. (Lk 23:44)**

It is here that we get a glimpse of the spiritual side of the Cross through the window of Psalms 22. The sixth hour is noon and the sun goes out. Not long after the words, "**To day shalt thou be with me in Paradise**" emanate from the torn, bloodied lips and swollen tongue of our Lord, the light goes out and it becomes very dark on Golgotha that day. The darkness includes

Four Sides of Calvary

the light of the sun going out. It is a cold, thick, creepy darkness that can be felt. It put tingling "goose bumps" on the bodies of those around the three crosses, and seems like their hair is standing up. The dreaded sense of evil swirls in the air and feels like the cold slick skin of snakes' bellies.

There is so much more to the darkness at this time. It is a darkness permitted by the Father, and it is a battle taking place between good and evil. All of Hell, with Satan in all of his fury, is seeking to destroy Jesus Christ. Oh, they hate Him as no others do. It is he that has ruined their plans, taken their power, and has sealed their fate. Though they do not believe that. They believe that they will ultimately win.

The soldiers, as well as Peter, John, Mary Magdalene, Mary and others are all astonished and taken with great fearful wonder. What is happening? They cannot see in the darkness. They can only listen and try to hear if Jesus speaks. The soldiers feel around for the torches and finally light them from the fire pit. Dim, yellow flickers of light dance in the darkness and illuminate three bloody naked figures nailed to crosses. The soldiers wonder why the torches do not seem as bright now for some reason? It is darker than midnight with no moon, but it is actually noon without the day light. And for three hours it stays that way.

Down, down, down, in the deepest recesses of Hell are the most powerful devils. The great villains of wickedness dwell amongst the damned as they burn in the black fire, their tortured screams filling the utter

Four Sides of Calvary

blackness of the abyss. They are chained in the prison of Hell and reserved in darkness for judgement at the Great White Throne. All of a sudden their prison doors snap open, and the power that bound them there is released.

They begin to laugh with a hideous, maniacal laughter that sounds like the deep angry growl of lions mixed with the blood thirsty howls of ravaging wolves. These "villains of Hell" look upward and begin to rise. All of Hell is watching, cheering and gnashing their teeth as they see them rise. All that is evil is watching as their strongest and fiercest warriors are heading to Golgotha to destroy the One they hate with a passion that is as strong as the fires of Hell itself. This is their chance to become free. The higher they rise the more their fury burns against the One who is hanging on the cross.

The bleachers of Hell begin to shake from the deep guttural roar of devils, along with the howls of wolves. The piercing screeches of black ravens is mixed with it as well, as all of Hell blasphemously cheers them on.

Hell is a place of no hope, but this day hope is found amongst the damned with the gleeful anticipation that these ascending warriors of Hell will win the battle and set them free. Higher and higher they rise until finally they come out of the pit smelling of the rotten egg odor of brimstone. These villains of Hell are furious that they have "unjustly" suffered in Hell fire. Now evil, furious vengeance explodes within them as they attack their enemy the Lord Jesus Christ.

Four Sides of Calvary

Bleeding in the darkness on Calvary, a multitude of fierce powerful devils referred to as the "bulls of Bashan," smash into the One that is all good. Yes, Jesus is highly outnumbered that dark day. He is all alone in this battle. All that is evil slams into all that is Holy. A battle is taking place like no other that had ever been fought.

> **8 He is near that justifieth me; who will contend with me? let us stand together: who is mine adversary? let him come near to me. (Is 50:8)**

The fight is on! Jesus challenged the devil and the fight is on.

> **11 Be not far from me; for trouble is near; for there is none to help.**
>
> **12 Many bulls have compassed me: strong bulls of Bashan have beset me round.**
>
> **13 They gaped upon me with their mouths, as a ravening and a roaring lion. (Ps 22:11-13)**

Here in Psalms 22 is a window of the spiritual battle that takes place. Jesus Christ is now covered with devils. They are the strongest devils in all of Hell. Bulls of Bashan, they are called.

There in the darkness, all of Hell collides with the beloved Son of God who is in the form of a man. When the spiritual battle fronts smash into each other, the physical body of Jesus Christ reels under the stress. From the evil force of the devils as they collide with our Lord, every joint in the body of Jesus Christ pops and

Four Sides of Calvary

all of His bones dislocate under the stress of it all. The physical stress of the Cross alone, though very great, would not cause all of His bones to dislocate. But the pressure from the spiritual battle causes the Lord Jesus Christ to have every bone pop out of joint.

> ^{14} I am poured out like water, and all my bones are out of joint... (Ps 22:14)
>
> ^{17} I may tell all my bones: they look and stare upon me. (Ps 22:17)

All of Hell watches, screams, and roars, in a most putrid fashion. The evil bulls of Bashan chew, puke, tear, rip, and attack Jesus Christ in ways we can't imagine. We have absolutely no idea the enormity of their attack. Our Lord Jesus Christ is covered with devils and He fights them as one man. No angels come to help Him. The Father does not step in to help Him either. Our Lord fights this battle in the darkness and all alone that day at the place of the skull known as Calvary.

It is very hard to be in a long, hot battle and sense that you are all alone. No one has come to help or stand by your side. Sometimes in these battles you may think that even God is not even aware of what you are going through. And usually in such times as this, you are worn out and have no strength left. It is like you are sinking and no longer have any strength to swim. In such times remember that Jesus understands more than you know, and what it is like to fight and suffer all alone.

In the midst of this battle at Calvary there is someone talking into our Lord's ear. It is Satan himself.

Four Sides of Calvary

²¹ Save me from the lion's mouth...(Ps 22:21)

Perhaps Satan speaks into His ear and says, *"You know this is a waste of time. Those people you are dying for. They don't love you. As a matter of fact, they hate you. You really ought to quit. All of this suffering you could end it all right now, go back to Heaven where you are praised and accepted. But these people don't love you and they don't care about you. They love me and serve me. You love them and show them you love them, and they don't care. I make them feel good, and they love me. Jesus,"* Satan hisses into His ear, *"You are wasting your time. Why don't you just quit!"*

Time passes. 12:30 p.m...., 1:00 p.m..., 1:30 p.m., darkness is still covering three crosses up on Golgotha.

All of Heaven stares down upon the Holy Lamb of God. The angels, cherubim, and the seraphim watch. Perhaps in silence they behold the One whom they have worshipped as He battles and dies on an old rugged cross.

The Bible says,

> **¹⁴ And as Moses lifted up the serpent in the wilderness, even so must the Son of man be lifted up:**
> **¹⁵ That whosoever believeth in him should not perish, but have eternal life.** (Jn 3:14-15)

I can understand Jesus being likened unto a lion, the Lion of the tribe of Judah. I can understand Jesus being likened unto a lamb, **"Behold the Lamb of God, which taketh away the sin of the world."** (Jn 1:29) I can

Four Sides of Calvary

understand Him being likened to bread: the Bread of Life. (Jn 6:48) I can understand him being likened unto water; "**...whosoever drinketh of the water that I shall give him shall never thirst...**" (Jn 4:14)

When I was lost, I was hungry and thirsty for something that satisfied. I can understand my Lord being likened to bread and water for I have taken and eaten of the Bread of Life. And I have drunk of the Water of Life. But I have a hard time understanding Jesus Christ being likened unto a serpent. That is what Satan was in the Garden of Eden. "**Now the serpent was more subtil than any beast of the field which the LORD God had made.**" (Gn 3:1)

The reference in John 3:14 is to Numbers 21:

> ^{4} And they journeyed from mount Hor by the way of the Red sea, to compass the land of Edom: and the soul of the people was much discouraged because of the way.
>
> ^{5} And the people spake against God, and against Moses, Wherefore have ye brought us up out of Egypt to die in the wilderness? for there is no bread, neither is there any water; and our soul loatheth this light bread.
>
> ^{6} And the LORD sent fiery serpents among the people, and they bit the people; and much people of Israel died.
>
> ^{7} Therefore the people came to Moses, and said, We have sinned, for we have spoken against the LORD, and against thee; pray

Four Sides of Calvary

> unto the LORD, that he take away the serpents from us. And Moses prayed for the people.
>
> ^{8} And the LORD said unto Moses, Make thee a fiery serpent, and set it upon a pole: and it shall come to pass, that every one that is bitten, when he looketh upon it, shall live.
>
> ^{9} And Moses made a serpent of brass, and put it upon a pole, and it came to pass, that if a serpent had bitten any man, when he beheld the serpent of brass, he lived. (Nm 21:4-9)

The children of Israel are dying. According to the orders from God, Moses makes a brass serpent and puts it upon a pole. He then holds it up, and all who had been bit from the serpents, when they look upon the brass serpent, they live. What is so amazing about the story is that the day Moses walked through Israel holding up that brass serpent, was a picture of the day that Jesus Christ would be held up on a wooden cross. That brasen serpent was a picture of Jesus Christ? How can that be?

> ^{21} For he hath made him to be sin for us, who knew no sin; that we might be made the righteousness of God in him. (2 Cor 5:21)

Here is another truly astonishing thing to think about. Jesus Christ, the Creator of all, could have easily gotten out of all of the suffering that He was going through, as well as the suffering that He still had to endure. Angels were ready to come to His aid. Yet willingly He continued in His suffering, alone on Calvary. To fully understand the love of God is not possible this side of Heaven.

The Bible says:

> [19] **And to know the love of Christ, which passeth knowledge...** (Eph 3:19)

I know that our Lord Jesus Christ loved His Father and came to do His Father's will; so He continued in his suffering. I know that our Lord loved you, dear reader, and He loved me when we were lost in sin and were enemies of God; so He willingly continued in His suffering. And I know that He was having the opportunity to exercise love, the greatest example and form of love that ever will be. He never would have been able to exercise this love, if He had not created the angels, cherubim, seraphim, and man with a free will.

Because God allowed for a free will, and thus the fall of all mankind, He was able to choose to love us, and allow us to choose to love Him back. And, in a most marvelous reality, God was able to love His enemies. It is absolutely amazing!

It gets down to this. How do you love a robot? If God is love, and He is, then there is a desire in God to exercise love. So the greatest opportunity to love is to die for your enemies and to pay for their sins.

This dark day on Calvary is the greatest picture of love the world will ever have. No other "god" is presented as, or comparable to the Lord Jesus Christ. The gods of this world are presented as tyrants with fierce anger. But here, shrouded in the darkness, yet for all the world to see as recorded in the word of God, is God's love for His creation. He loved the world, when the world hated him!

> **^{16} For God so loved the world, that he gave his only begotten Son, that whosoever believeth in him should not perish, but have everlasting life. (Jn 3:16)**
>
> **^{6} For when we were yet without strength, in due time Christ died for the ungodly.**
>
> **^{7} For scarcely for a righteous man will one die: yet peradventure for a good man some would even dare to die.**
>
> **^{8} But God commendeth his love toward us, in that, while we were yet sinners, Christ died for us. (Rom 5:6-8)**

Jesus Christ is going to battle for you and for me. He is fighting a battle that you and I would never be able to fight. He is paying the price you and I could never pay. Oh, what a Saviour! And what a battle it is!

His tongue is cleaving to His jaws. He is dehydrated. All of His bones are out of joint. His blood is still flowing out of the shredded flesh of His body. Parts of His body are now extremely black and blue from the bruising. Blood has dried in His hair and on His body. His soul has become sin. The very opposite of all that God is, for God is holy. Becoming sin; my sin and your sin, has to be one of the most disgusting experiences that happens to Him while He is on the Cross. But it is not the worst experience to Him. The worst, which comes

Four Sides of Calvary

later, makes Him shout out from the cross.

He is being provoked and harassed by the bulls of Bashan. If this taunting and attack from them upon our Saviour were allowed upon you and me, we would soon be crushed. We would end up in a hospital in pain for the rest of our earthly lives where pain medication couldn't even touch it.

Yet, Jesus Christ is abiding the suffering. Because He is abiding so well, the bulls of Bashan become more and more frustrated. They strike with all of their might, harder, faster, meaner, yet He withstands their onslaught as an eagle in the sky that is harassed by a few small black birds.

With His Son suffering in the darkness on earth, the angels ask again to go deliver Jesus Christ, but the Father makes no reply. He with all the rest of Heaven continue to watch. Then something begins to happen. Angels gasp in unbelief. They look to the Father on His throne as He shines brighter than the sun. The angels, with wonder and amazement they've never experienced before cry out, *"No, no, it can't be! Father, do something!"*

Then, in the darkness on Golgotha that day, Jesus Christ begins to change. He becomes sin for you and me. Jesus Christ becomes a serpent and the very embodiment of sin. In John 3:14 and Psalms 22, as well as having Numbers 21 as the example, there is no doubt that Jesus Christ became a worm for you and me.

> ^{6} But I am a worm, and no man... (Ps 22:6)
>
> ^{14} And as Moses lifted up the serpent in the wilderness, even so must the Son of man be lifted up... (Jn 3:14)

If Jesus Christ is taking the sinner's place as a substitutionary sacrifice, and if sinners turn into the lowest form of life when they reach Hell, **"Where their worm dieth not, and the fire is not quenched"** (Mk 9:44), then Jesus Christ became a worm for you and me. He became the personification of sin. Yes, He took my sin, He bore my sin, and He became my sin. Absolutely amazing, isn't it! This is something we need to stop and ponder for a while.

Jesus not only becomes sin for you and me, but He suffers the agonies of Hell as He hangs on the Cross.

The Passover Lamb was to be roast with fire. When Jesus, vicariously through David, says in Psalms 22 **"I am a worm,"** as well as he says **"I thirst,"** as well as **"my God my God, why hast thou forsaken me?"** those are the cries of the damned in Hell. The suffering of Christ as sin, and for sin, takes place on the cross. Once he says, **"It is finished,"** then it is finished.

There are brethren who claim that Jesus suffered in Hell after he died on the Cross. They get this by considering the fact that Jesus came to die in the sinner's place. And that is true. But after he proclaims, it is finished, then his suffering is done. The atonement is completed, and his suffering is over.

> ^{5} But he was wounded for our transgressions, he was bruised for our

iniquities: the chastisement of our peace was upon him; and with his stripes we are healed.

⁶ All we like sheep have gone astray; we have turned every one to his own way; and the LORD hath laid on him the iniquity of us all. (Is 53:5-6)

²⁴ Who his own self bare our sins in his own body on the tree... (1 Pt 2:24)

Not long ago I heard a true story about a missionary meeting in Papua, New Guinea. It was to be a big meeting with some pastors coming all the way from the United States of America. Great preparations were made as the Christian natives were very excited about seeing and hearing the pastors of the missionary men who had been ministering to them in Papua, New Guinea over the years.

The pastors arrived and were lodged in the best houses in all of the area. There were four dimensional frame, timber houses where they stayed. These four houses had indoor plumbing. For the area, I assume, it was very fancy compared to the way the common people lived. In the houses, the bathroom pipes drained into underground pipes that drained the sewage into a central, covered pit. The sewage then leached out through other pipes into the leach field.

During the meeting the pipes backed up into the houses with sewage. When the natives found out they were troubled in a good way and immediately set out to fix the problem. (It seems like something always goes wrong in special meetings.)

Four Sides of Calvary

The men went to the central pit, where all the sewage flowed into and pulled back the covering. Then one of the men stepped over the edge of that pit and got right into the raw smelly sewage. (Have you ever been around raw toilet sewage?) And if that wasn't bad enough, he then submerged himself completely under the sewage and reached the entrance of the pipe that was all covered with weeds and sticks, thus blocking the proper flow of the sewage. He fixed it by clearing the debris away from the mouth of the pipe so the sewage could once again flow out and leach into the ground. All the while he was submerged under the raw, deadly, smelly sewage. (That man has some gold laid up in Heaven! No doubt, he did that for Jesus Christ.) But the thought of being submerged under sewage, with nothing over your mouth, just holding your breath, is enough to make you gag!

But I know a story of a Saviour-our Lord Jesus Christ. And He did not just submerge himself into sin. He became sin for you and me. It is one thing to submerge yourself into sewage, but it is another to become that sewage!!! Jesus Christ became sin for you and I. There on the Cross He became sin.

[21] **For he hath made him to be sin for us...(2 Cor 5:21)**

Time drags on: 1:30p.m..., 2:00p.m. The darkness remains. In the physical realm, it seems like not much is happening. The darkness to those on Golgatha is obviously strange. But the centurions' torches burn and cast dim light upon the crosses. Other than that,

Four Sides of Calvary

some conversations between the soldiers take place, but not much else.

The centurion, along with Peter, John, Mary Magdalene, Mary, and others listen in the darkness. They hear gasps and groans from the other two men, but no sound is uttered from Jesus Christ. He is "**...as a sheep before her shearers...**" (Is 53:7) The disciples and women, their minds confused and their hearts broken, peer through the darkness to see the Lord. To them, this is the end of the road. Their Messiah, their leader, their friend, He is dying, and they have no answers as to why or to where they go from here? It is a very somber sorrowful atmosphere at the foot of the three crosses.

In the spiritual realm though, down, down below in the pit of Hell they are panicking. All of their forces, the torture, the pain, and stress inflicted on Jesus Christ are not making any progress against the Son of God. His body is disfigured and contorted from all the bones being out of joint, yet Jesus remains steadfast and faithful to His Father, the word of God, and for you and me. Calling upon all that is available, down in Hell the "second string, the reserves" are called upon to augment and help out the bulls of Bashan. It is time to call out the dogs.

> [15] **My strength is dried up like a potsherd; and my tongue cleaveth to my jaws; and thou hast brought me into the dust of death.**
> [16] **For dogs have compassed me...**
> **(Ps 22:15-16)**

20 **Deliver my soul from the sword; my darling from the power of the dog. (Ps 22:20)**

I remember talking to a man one day who had been attending my church. As we talked, the subject of Hell came up and the gates of Hell.

When I mentioned the gates of Hell, he looked at me with a very serious expression and said, *"You know, Hell has gates."*

I replied, *"Yes, it does."*

He looked at me kind of surprised that I agreed with him, and said to me, *"Do you believe that Hell has gates?"*

To which I again replied, *"Yes, it does. That is what the Bible says."*

He then said, with a look of fear in his eyes, and a little stutter in his words *"T...T...There are dogs at those gates, b...b...but they're not like the dogs we know."*

I then replied, *"Yes, there are dogs there, and I am sure they are not like the dogs we know."*

Again, he looked quite surprised at me that I believed him. I then took him to Psalm 22 and showed him the reference to the dogs. He then told me the following story.

He said that he had grown up in San Fransisco. As he became a teenager, in a broken home, and a hard family with a lot of booze going around, he ended up getting into drugs: hard drugs. On one of his drug trips, he said he saw the gates of Hell. I could tell, just the memory of the "vision" brought it all back to him like it was yesterday. It is similar to when soldiers recount battles, and when they do, all of the emotions return as well.

Did he actually see the gates of Hell? I don't know, but I do know that what he told me lined up with what the word of God says. There are references in the Bible to dogs in the spirit world. He also told me that it wasn't too long after that bad drug trip that he got saved. I am sure a glimpse of Hell would sober up a lot of people.

As a last ditch effort to stop the Lord Jesus Christ, the dogs of Hell are unleashed. They too ascend and with a hatred, a rabid hatred for Jesus Christ, they begin to attack. Jesus Christ is now covered with devils from head to foot. They also chew, tear, puke, and do unspeakable atrocities to the King of Glory. There in the darkness Jesus is suffering, bleeding dying, and fighting the battle you and I could never fight. He is fighting for our survival.

Who is this? This is the Father's beloved Son. This is the Creator of the universe. This is the Man that raised the dead, healed the lepers, and held the children in His arms. This is the Man that fed the multitudes. And this is the Man that never sinned. He is Holy, Holy, Holy, the Lord God Almighty. Almighty? Yes! Yet He is dying a slow painful death.

All of Heaven is still watching in wonder and amazement. They don't understand. The Father continues to behold "**...the travail of His soul.**" (Is 53:11)

The time is somewhere around 2:45 in the afternoon. It has now been over five and a half hours since Jesus Christ was nailed to the Cross. It has been dark since

Four Sides of Calvary

noon. There has not been much sound around the three crosses. Suddenly a voice pierces the calm like a wild crack of thunder which shakes the soldiers, the disciples and the women.

> ²⁸ **After this, Jesus knowing that all things were now accomplished, that the scripture might be fulfilled, saith, I thirst.**
> (Jn 19:28)

Do you see that? **"Jesus knowing that all things were now accomplished..."** Can you behold that all Jesus Christ is going through, yet, according to this verse, in His agony Jesus is reviewing, making sure He has accomplished all that the Father sent Him to do. The presence of His mind is not on Himself.

Jesus, making sure that all things were accomplished, in so many words said, *"He'll be alright now. She'll be alright now."* Who? Dear reader, do you see that when the Bible says, **"...knowing that all things were now accomplished..."** it is showing you that the Lord had you on His heart and mind. You and me! He could rest then, for the price had been paid, and all who want Him as their Saviour can freely accept Him now. He saw you as He hung on that Cross, and while He was dying He made sure He had finished His job so that you could get saved and join Him in Heaven one day. Oh, what a Saviour!

Once he knows all is done, he speaks and says, **"I thirst."** Again, this is the cry of souls in Hell, for the rich man in Luke 16 asks for water to cool his tongue. It can also be the cry of a thirst for His Father. **"As the**

Four Sides of Calvary

hart panteth after the water brooks, so panteth my soul after thee, O God." (Ps 42:1)

At Calvary the trinity was never broken, and Jesus Christ was always God manifest in the flesh. Jesus was fully God all the way.

Jesus is crying out for his father when he says, "**I thirst.**"

Mary Magdalene jumps up in the darkness. Torches blaze and cast dancing golden yellow flickers of light to dimly illuminate the three bodies hanging upon the rough-cut, wooden crosses. She stares at Jesus intently listening and looking for any more activity. Then Peter and John also jump up.

John asks Peter and Mary, *"What did he say?"*

One of the soldiers speaks and says, *"I think he said he was thirsty."* He then gives the Lord a drink of vinegar.

Have you ever had vinegar spill into a cut? It stings harshly! There is a strong stinging around the Lord's mouth as the vinegar is given.

> ^{28} **After this, Jesus knowing that all things were now accomplished, that the scripture might be fulfilled, saith, I thirst.**
>
> ^{29} **Now there was set a vessel full of vinegar: and they filled a spunge with vinegar, and put it upon hyssop, and put it to his mouth.**
>
> ^{30} **When Jesus therefore had received the vinegar...** (Jn 19:28-30)

The atonement has been made. Now He is given vinegar, so our Lord receives the vinegar. It is not the

Four Sides of Calvary

gall, which contained water, as was put before Him in the early minutes of the Crucifixion.

Minutes pass as disciples and others peer and listen in the darkness. All that can be heard are groans and cries coming from the other two on either side of Jesus Christ.

Then a loud cry that could be heard all the way down in Jerusalem, rings out and breaks the silence, like the thunderous roar of a lion at night, **"My God, my God, why hast thou forsaken me?"** (Mt 27:46) Jesus has prayed to His Father, **"I thirst."** Father, I want you. And there, in the thick darkness on Calvary, for almost six hours, a forsaking has taken place. It is not a dividing of the trinity that took place at Calvary. Nor was it an emptying of the Diety out of the body of Jesus Christ. But it is a silence. The Father has been silent; until this moment.

See the scene one more time. Physically, Jesus Christ has every bone out of joint. His tongue cleaves to the roof of His mouth. His stripes, the nails through His hands and feet, as well as His thorny crown and torn off beardless cheeks are all still bleeding. Almost all of his blood is gone.

Spiritually, Jesus is covered with devils, and they are doing all they can to get him to fail or quit. All of Hell is watching, shouting, roaring as they watch the Son of God being attacked. He is making a show of them openly. They are losing, and losing badly.

The Father, according to Jesus Christ, has forsaken Him. Jesus cries out and the Father restores His fellowship to his beloved Son and then says, *"That is enough!"*

¹¹ **He shall see of the travail of his soul, and shall be satisfied...** (Is 53:11)

How much the Father watched before the forsaking, I have no idea. But I do know from Isaiah 53:11 that the Father saw "...the travail of his soul..." and was satisfied. The Father's will was accomplished, which was the Son's desire to do.

Jesus said in Psalm 22:21 **"Save me from the lion's mouth: for thou hast heard me from the horns of the unicorns."** In this verse it is the Lord praying to the Father while He is on the Cross, and mentions the unicorns. In Heaven there are creatures called unicorns. I know from various scriptures that they are very powerful.

⁹ **Will the unicorn be willing to serve thee, or abide by thy crib?**
¹⁰ **Canst thou bind the unicorn with his band in the furrow? or will he harrow the valleys after thee?** (Jb 39:9-10)

These verses show that a unicorn is stronger than Satan himself. In the context of Job 39, God is asking the Devil these questions. No, the unicorn is not willing to serve the Devil. And no, Satan cannot bind the unicorn. With these scriptures we can see that the unicorn is a very powerful creature. The Bible speaks of unicorns that are present at the second advent of Jesus Christ in Isa. 34:7. They shall come down with the rest of the saints that return to this earth and take over at the start of the Millennium.

Our Lord is praying and mentions the unicorns. The efforts of the devils to defeat Jesus Christ are not working. And I am sure that the devils that were upon Jesus Christ would not be willing to stop and say, *"Well boys, it looks like we lost. It's time for us to go back to Hell."* I just don't think they would do that, especially since Hell is the place of the rebellious for all time.

Obviously, Jesus Christ at this point has not resurrected from the grave. He is still in a body of flesh and still in the battle. So I wonder, I am not sure of this though, but I wonder if God the Father up in Heaven, looks over at the unicorns and says, *"Go take those devils off of him."* And that is just the command they are waiting for. With the power of God, "the cavalry is coming" and upon reaching the Cross they use their horn to rip and remove the devils off of Jesus Christ. The battle is over and Jesus Christ has won.

When Jesus cries out, **"My God, My God, why hast thou forsaken me?"** (Mt 27:46), one of the soldiers can't understand what He is saying and thinks that He is calling for Elijah. He gives Him some vinegar and Jesus takes some. Why now and not before? The payment has been made, and yet the first liquid was gall, but here it is vinegar. There is no water in the vinegar.

Another soldier speaks up and says, *"Leave him alone. Let's see whether Elijah will come."*

And then just before 3:00p.m. that Wednesday afternoon, Jesus speaks some marvelous words for us sinners. **"It is finished."** The bulls of Bashan and the dogs are gone. The suffering is over because the

Four Sides of Calvary

complete payment has been made. There is no need for our Lord to go and suffer in Hell. He has taken the sinners' place as their substitute offering. The payment has been made. Salvation is now free. Jesus said, **"It is finished,"** and therefore it is finished! The perfect sacrifice has been made.

Not long after those words, Jesus says, **"Father, into thy hands, I commend my Spirit."** (Lk 23:46)

With that said, He bows his head, gives up the ghost, and leaves His earthly body.

Suddenly, in the darkness, a rumbling of the ground begins, and an earthquake begins to shake the ground. The crosses begin to jerk back and forth, and the other two men scream out in pain. Someone can be heard yelling out, *"It's an earthquake!"* The people standing around the crosses crouch down to the ground.

The earthquake shakes all of Jerusalem. And inside the temple something amazing happens. The beautiful, thick, strong blue, purple and scarlet (Ex 26:31) vail that separated the Holy Place from the Holiest Of All, is rent in twain, from the top to the bottom. The Father reaches down from Heaven and says, *"I won't be needing this anymore."*

Now the way into the Holiest of all is through the Lamb of God, the Lord Jesus Christ. No more shall man need to go through a priest. If man wants to access the Father, then he must go directly through the Son, Jesus Christ. It is now a personal and an individual access.

The sun comes out and begins to shine once again.

Four Sides of Calvary

The ground ceases to rumble and shake. Slowly people stand upon their feet. With squinty eyes because of the dark, they now stare at that One in the middle.

Mary Magdalene takes a long stare at the body, and then speaks to Peter with a trembling, broken, and fearful voice as she desperately cries, *"Peter....he...he's..not moving!"* Tears begin to flow out of her eyes, *"He's not moving. He's not breathing. Oh no, Peter, He's gone."* As the words come off her lips, she buries her face in her hands and weeps.

Beside the crosses is the centurion, who has been watching the whole time. He also has heard of Jesus Christ and the wonderful works that He has done. With a serious look on his face, but speaking not much above a whisper he says as if to himself, **"Certainly this was a righteous man."** (Lk 23:47) He pauses for a few minutes of contemplation, and then proclaims emphatically so all can hear, **"Truly, this was the Son of God."** (Mt 27:54)

The disciples look at each other in confusion, for they still do not understand what it is all about.

Below the cross in the underworld, Jesus descends down, down, down into the pit of Hell. He has some unfinished business to do. Part of that business is to dump the sins of the universe into the pit of Hell. Hell is such a dirty place!

As He approaches, the gates of Hell swing open to Him and He enters. After dumping our sins there, He begins to preach and basically says this:

"You all thought that you would win. You thought, and some of you even still think that you have me. Well, I just

want you to know that your damnation is now sealed. You have no hope. Your judgement is settled, and you are just waiting for the sentencing which will come at the Great White Throne Judgement."

With that He turns and walks towards the gates. There at those gates is the gate keeper. He is called Death, and proclaims, *"No one gets out of here. Well..., almost no one. There was one man years ago by the name of Jonah, but he was an exception."*

Jesus then reaches over and takes the keys from him. The keys of Death and Hell. With that, He brakes out of the prison of Hell. The gates of Hell could not prevail against the Rock, our Lord Jesus Christ. He was on the other side of the gates of Hell; but they could not keep Him in.

He then crosses over the great gulf that separates Hell from Paradise and enters Paradise, where the saints of the Old Testament are staying. Loud cheers arise that could be heard clear over in Hell. Then Jesus proclaims, *"I know you all have been waiting for me. The blood has been shed, the price has been paid. Are you ready to go home?"*

With that they start shouting *"Glory to the Lamb of God! Hallelujah to the Lamb! We are going home!"*

Three days and three nights passed. Very early in the morning, before one could know another, Jesus arises from the dead. As they say, *"You can't keep a good man down!"* The One that defeated death arose.

After appearing to Mary first, He then leads all of Paradise up to Heaven.

> Up from the grave He arose,
> With a mighty triumph o'er His foes;
> He arose a victor from the dark domain,
> And He lives forever with His saints to reign:
> He arose! He arose!
> Hallelujah! Christ arose!

It has been over thirty-three years since the Son of God has sat on the right hand of the Father. Heaven was never the same without Him there. He left that throne with a pure and perfect body. After all, this is God the Son, the Most High God, He is perfect and his body was perfect. The wait is finally over and Jesus is now coming home.

Forty days earlier he had led the way with all of the saints of Paradise following behind Him. Entering "...**by his own blood he entered in once into the holy place, having obtained eternal redemption for us.**" (Heb 9:12) Jesus Christ led the way, and behind him came Paradise with all of its saints. As they entered Heaven, they shouted praises to the Lamb that was slain. It was a new kind of praise that had never been heard in Heaven before. There was an emotion, a thankfulness that had never been sensed in Heaven before. It was the thankful, joyful praise that comes from those who know that if they had received what they deserve, they would be down, down below in Hell. But here they are, with wonder and amazement, that they made it to Heaven.

Four Sides of Calvary

Now, forty days later, the Son is coming home. He is coming as the triumphant King that He truly is. All of the angels and celestial beings stand and line the brightly beaming, crystal clear, beautiful golden street that leads straight up to God's holy throne. With them are the saints of old, shouting and praising the Lamb of God.

It is finished! The battle is over! King Jesus has won, and Heaven's King is now coming home. The glories and the shouts of praise are louder than they have ever been before. There is great joy that fills all as He passes before them on His way to the throne to sit down at the right hand of the Father. His eyes are bright with power and glory. His hair is whiter than new fallen snow. His garments cover His body, but glory beams out from under it at His feet, His wrists and His neck. He is altogether lovely. This is their King. Glory to God in the Highest, He is home! But something strange takes place as He passes.

The angels begin to stare at Him, but more specifically, they stare at His hands and feet. Their praise still sounds out, yet they are distracted as they shout. Their eyes see something that wasn't there thirty-three years earlier. On the Lamb of God are scars in His hands and feet. The King of Heaven is not the same as when He left. His body is now scarred.

It is a strange thing to think about, but when our Lord Jesus Christ left Heaven, He and His body were perfect without spot and blemish. Yet the Bible says:

> ^{10} **For it became him, for whom are all things, and by whom are all things, in bringing many sons unto glory, to make the captain of their salvation perfect through sufferings.** (Heb 2:10)

Jesus was made perfect through sufferings, that he might taste death for every man. It is something to think about. After Calvary, God's eternal glorified body had changed. His body now had eternal scars in it. A reminder? No, God does not forget. No, those scars are a glory and a testament to an act that God never would have been able to exercise if He had not created all of the beings in Heaven and earth with a free will. They are a testament to what God could do because He allowed for a fall and rebellion to take place. He was able to exercise, and experience love. God is love, and in Heaven He has scars in His body that will always remain a testament to the love of God. I wonder if our Lord at times will look at His scars, and then just smile?

As the angels gather around the throne, they stare at those scars on His hands, and then at His feet. Perhaps He says to them, look here, and pulls His robe up and there is the scar from the spear that pierced His side. With wonder they are silent and don't know what to do.

After a while a man comes through the crowd up to the throne, and his name is Sampson. As he sees the scars in the hands of Jesus Christ he begins to shout *"Glory to God!!! Halellujah!!! Whooooo hoooo!!!"* And runs off praising God. The angels look at one another with a strange look.

Four Sides of Calvary

Then some more saints come through the throng and see the scars on his hands and feet, and they start shouting and praising the Lamb of God as well. Then a man comes through the crowd. The Bible never gives his name. He looks at the scars, and then looks up at the face of His Lord. With joy he falls on his knees and worships the Lamb with praise like no other. Who is that man? Ah, me thinks it is the dying thief. He falls to his knees and thanks the Lord for rescuing him at the last moment.

I heard a true story years ago of a mother who always wore gloves. They would be very pretty gloves. Sometimes white, sometimes other colors, but she always wore gloves. Her daughter, who was in her early teens one day came into the bedroom, where her mother was sitting at her bedroom vanity getting ready to go out. The young girl had entered so quietly that her mother, who was facing the mirror, had not noticed. Her mother had not put her gloves on yet. The daughter walked up beside her and saw her mother's badly discolored and deformed hands.

As her mother realized she was not alone quickly tried to put her gloves on. The young girl stopped her and softly asked, *"Momma, what happened? Why do you always where those gloves?"*

Her mother, knowing she could not keep it a secret any longer, told her the following story.

"When you were just a few months old, we had a horrible fire and the house burned down. When I realized the house was on fire I ran into your bedroom.

Four Sides of Calvary

All around your crib was on fire, but I did not stop. I reached through the fire, covered you in a blanket and brought you out of the fire safe. But my hands were severely burned through it all. I have kept them in gloves so people don't see how ugly and deformed they are."

The young girl, now knowing the story, reached out and for the first time in her life she held and stared at her mother's fire-scarred hands. Realizing the greatness and sacrifice of her mother's love, she tenderly leaned over and kissed them. Then looking into her mother's eyes she softly said, *"Oh Momma. Those are not ugly hands. Those are the most beautiful hands in all of the world to me."*

Our Lord has nail-scarred hands and feet, and a hole in His side. Yet, to me, there is no doubt that those are the most beautiful scars I will ever see.

Notes

List of works by the Author

All works are available through online stores, such as Amazon, Books-A-Million, Google books, etc.

All works are also available through physical stores such as Barnes & Noble, Books-A-Million etc.

1. **Here Comes the Bride**, A Critique of the Baptist Bride Heresy. 174 pages

2. **Good Vibrations**, Overcoming Spasmodic Dysphonia, 218 Pages

3. **Defiled**, The Spiritual Dangers of Alternative Medicine, 351 pages

4. **Aromatherapy**, From a Biblical Perspective, 236 pages

Sermon in a Book Series

1. **Jesus, Talk to Me**, Have You Ever Desired to Get the Lord's attention?, 54 Pages

2. **Dealing with Bad In-laws**, A Bible study on Jacob and Laban, 116 Pages

3. **EVEN AS GOD**, Healing relationships Biblically, 190 Pages

4. **FOUR SIDES OF CALVARY**, Our Lord's Battle on the Cross, 84 Pages

5. **THE SONS OF ZADOK**, What will You do for 1000 Years?, 184 pages